*Evening**Express**

ABERDEEN
Memories
A Hidden Archive Uncovered

compiled by RAYMOND ANDERSON

D0317542

DB PUBLISHING

First published in Great Britain in 2000 by The Breedon Books Publishing Company Limited, 3 The Parker Centre, Derby, DE21 4SZ.

This paperback edition published in Great Britain in 2011 by The Derby Books Publishing Company Limited, 3 The Parker Centre, Derby, DE21 4SZ.

ISBN 978-1-908234-01-8

Printed and bound by Melita Press, Malta

Contents

Introduction

IN this the third book I've produced for the *Evening Express* on the photographic history of Aberdeen and the North-East the emphasis has changed.

Instead of using Aberdeen Journals' pictures from the past I have great pleasure in showing many photographs from the readers of the Memories features – the 'hidden archive' of this book's title.

These are the photographs which have been lying half forgotten in drawers gaining interest and importance as the decades passed. Consider, for instance, the pictures used of men and women at work. Many of these hard industrial jobs have gone forever. The dress and demeanour of the boss in his hat and the workers and apprentices in these pictures reflect times which have past. And if there is a mission in this book it is that – to uncover these pictures from the past and reveal them to a wider audience. To store up the images which show where we have come from. Sadly, for every one picture preserved there are likely to be dozens lost.

This time, thanks to that huge resource the readers of the *Evening Express*, I have been able to fill in something of the stories behind the pictures we publish. I hope readers find them as interesting as I did when the letters and phone calls with snippets of information first arrived at my desk.

One whole chapter is devoted to the work of freelance photographer Leonard Pelman who worked in Aberdeen before World War Two. A large collection of his work was stored by retired Aberdeen businessman Jack Pirrie in those dark and difficult days before the outbreak of war. Unlike many at that time Jack appreciated the worth of this record of our area. I am particularly in debt to Leonard Pelman's daughter Joyce Pelella in New York State who has been so helpful in her backing for this project and in filling in the stories behind her dad's pictures.

The Pelman collection is an important body of work from a talented and energetic photographer always seeking a unique slant on events.

Of course it is not just individuals who can provide pictures from the past. Aberdeen Harbour Board's collection of thousands of glass prints being archived and put on the Internet by Aberdeen University as I write is a fine example of the importance now placed on our heritage. That project's important work is recognised in these pages.

And the *Evening Express* also has its old glass slides which have been hidden from the public for too long.

The enthusiasts of the Great North of Scotland Railway Association have also built up an impressive collection of pictures which deserve as wide an audience as possible.

But every single worthwhile photographic record of our past should be cherished and I hope this book acts as a spur for folk to rummage about and find those long overlooked pictures.

By its very nature this book cannot be a comprehensive collection. Rather, it is a jumble of pieces in a jigsaw puzzle of our history. Incomplete, but fascinating.

Raymond Anderson
July 2000

Pelman

SOME of the most interesting photographs in this book are the work of freelance photographer Leonard Pelman. More than 60 years – and a World War – since he worked in Aberdeen his daughter, Joyce Pelella, made contact with me from New York State.

This followed the publication of one of her father's pictures which had been stored by Jack Pirrie who ran his silk screen business from an office next to Leonard's in Adelphi Court.

Since then I have corresponded with Joyce over the Internet and learned much more about her father's distinguished career.

Joyce still has fond recollections of the exciting days when her father was a photographer in Aberdeen in the Thirties.

She says: "I am sure many married couples in their 70s and 80s still have wedding pictures which were taken by my father."

She also recalls her father's pioneering newsreels in Aberdeen. Short items for the News Cinema in Diamond Street. Joyce says: "The big heavy Bell & Howell movie camera was quite a thing to lug around."

Although only a young girl then, she says: "I can still remember most happenings, like the time when Ramsay MacDonald, the then Prime Minister, was up in Lossiemouth and carried my father across a river because he was wearing waders and my father wasn't."

Many other famous people were met by her photographer father in those times.

"There was Sir Malcolm Campbell racing his record-breaking car *Bluebird* at Cruden Bay sands, and Bobby Jones, founder of the Augusta Masters and one of golf's legendary figures, playing at Cruden Bay golf course," she told me.

"I used to like him covering the royals when they were on Deeside as I would be excited about the wild chase over the Devil's Elbow with the photos which were going to Glasgow. I was always bouncing around in the badly-sprung back seat of the Singer car.

"Life has never been quite as exciting as it was in those days," says Joyce.

After leaving Aberdeen in the late Thirties, Leonard Pelman worked in Fleet Street with the *Daily Express*, then the Press Association and Reuters before joining the Royal Navy where he worked as a photographer and covered the Dieppe landing.

Joyce married an American Air Force pilot in 1944 and moved to the USA, with her parents following in 1946.

The Pelmans settled in Portland, Oregon, for a few years before moving to New York State where the climate was considered healthier.

Leonard, the grandson and son of master portrait photographers, latterly worked for the New York Orange County Press.

Leonard's health began to fail and he died of a heart attack in 1959, aged 59.

Joyce told me: "He would be very flattered to think that he was remembered – I think he felt he was completely forgotten when he came over to the States and he eventually turned away from photography entirely."

Joyce Pelman in a picture taken by her father at Aberdeen's ancient Timmer Market where the tradition of selling timmer, or timber, toys developed.

Leonard Pelman and his car at Aberdeen Beach.

A picture of Joyce Pelman as a mature woman.

The Isles band at Aberdeen's Beach Ballroom in the Thirties. *Evening Express* readers recalled with pleasure the big bands which played there on Sunday nights. Entrance cost half-a-crown (12.5p) and only tea, coffee or soft drinks were served to the crowds who thronged there.

The biggest hole in Europe. Aberdeen's Rubislaw Quarry in the 1930s when the granite which built Aberdeen was still being hewn from the faces of the quarry.

Aberdeen's gateway to the world in the 1930s when the harbour was already a bustling and vital area of the city.

Processing becomes mechanised at one of Aberdeen's fish houses.

The Beauty of Marischal College. A Leonard Pelman aerial shot which won recognition from the Scottish National Salon in March 1933. The area around Aberdeen's granite masterpiece has now changed almost beyond recognition.

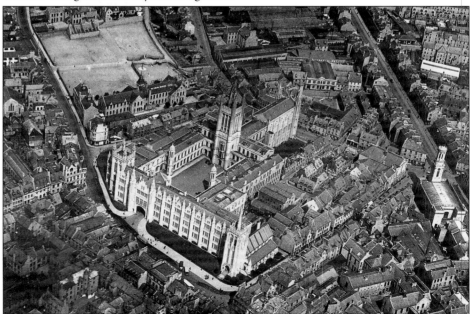

The *Aberdonian* steam train, a symbol of power and speed in the Thirties.

The ceremony to mark the laying of the foundation stone for a Robert Gordon's College building in Aberdeen – possibly a swimming pool – around 1928. On the extreme right is Bob Duguid, a photographer with the *Bon-Accord* and *Northern Pictorial* publications. Behind him is John Skene, the then Town Sergeant.

The picture which created one of the biggest reactions the Memories column in the *Evening Express* ever prompted. The appearance of the *Graf Zeppelin* airship over the North-East of Scotland in August 1939. Each writer had their own memory of that day but one reader had actually recorded what he had seen. George Gordon of King's Crescent, Aberdeen, was 23 years old at the time. He wrote: 'I was up at Craigiebuckler when I noticed this cigar-shaped object seemingly hanging in the sky far out at sea. I watched it on and off for about half-an-hour …I was on high ground with a wonderful view. It was only when I got home and saw the *Evening Express* that I discovered I had seen the *Graf Zeppelin*.' Mr Gordon continues: 'It was a moment of history. I was 23 at the time and a war that would intimately involve my generation was only a month away.'

The *Graf Zeppelin* pictured over Bridge of Don.

One of the North-East's lighthouses gets some attention to ensure it carries out its vital function over the winter months of 1938. It was absolutely essential that its life-saving light functioned perfectly.

The trawler *North Queen of Granton* aground at Whitelinks Bay, south of Inverallochy. The Fraserburgh fire brigade rescued the ten crew by breeches buoy in this early 1930s sea drama.

The Aberdeen trawler *Ben Strome* which ran aground on the Skerry Rock near Peterhead Bay. When the Peterhead Lifeboat reached the trawler in the early morning of 6 January 1934, the boat had been refloated by the rising tide. It was towed to Peterhead where it was beached with the Harbour Master's permission. Skipper E. Rae was almost trapped by the trawler rolling over with the cabin door jammed shut by the pressure of water. Skipper Rae said: "It was an anxious moment before the trawler heeled over in the other direction and I was able to scramble free."

The Aberdeen trawler the *Struan* which ran aground on the dreaded rocks of Scotstonhead on 19 January 1933. The crew of nine – who set fire to bedding to alert the rescue services after all their distress flares had been used – were rescued by what was described in the *Evening Express* as: 'One of Peterhead Lifeboat's most gallant feats of a long and glorious record.' The reporter on the spot wrote: 'The boat was urged through boiling seas, past cruel reefs' to the stricken trawler. Then four miles north of Peterhead the crew leaped to safety on to the lifeboat in a remarkable feat of seamanship which required the finest judgement by the lifeboatmen.

Leonard Pelman captures the terrible power of the sea during the fierce blizzard and storm of February 1933 which caused many safety alerts and rescues at sea and on land.

Aberdeen harbour packed with steam trawlers in the 1930s.

The huge crowds which gathered at Bay of Nigg after the trawler *Ben Screel* ran aground on 18 January 1933. All the crew were rescued with drivers helping by directing their headlights on the scene.

The *Ben Screel* stuck fast on the rocks at Bay of Nigg.

It was hard work, hauling baskets of fish aboard lorries at Aberdeen harbour.

All that remained of the Aberdeen trawler *Venetia* after she ran aground on the rocks at Cowie Point, Stonehaven, with loss of all nine crew. The tragedy happened unseen during a fierce gale on 2 January 1933. The alarm was raised by a farm servant who noticed wreckage on the shore. The worst fears were confirmed when lifebuoys were washed ashore with the words – 'Venetia, Aberdeen'.

Members of Aberdeen Curling Club pictured playing their first game of the season at Cults in the Thirties. On the left, I am informed, is Ian Cameron, a well-known local cricketer of the time.

Prime Minister Winston Churchill waves to surprised citizens as he tours war damaged Berlin in this picture Pelman took during World War Two.

Study in strength and concentration as a farm worker wrestles with a horse-drawn plough.

The Aberdeen Beach area in the 1930s when there was a variety theatre, a cafe, swimming pool, the Beach Ballroom and very little else.

Motorbike racing at Cruden Bay in 1932.

An evocative study of the Hall Russell yard in December 1938.

A placid scene is reflected on still waters at Aberdeen Harbour in the 1930s.

Aberdeen harbour as seen from the sea before high-rise buildings changed the skyline.

The elegant Palace Hotel on Aberdeen's Union Street which burned down in 1941.

The Palace Hotel, Aberdeen, pictured in the 1920s.

The Dutch giant Arthur and his little partner Sep on a visit to Aberdeen. The normal sized man on the right is a good comparison for the 9ft 3in Arthur.

Prime Minister Ramsay MacDonald in his home town of Lossiemouth.

A magnificent view of Aberdeen and a Tiger Moth of the Aberdeen University Air Squadron. This shot would have been taken with the aid of a box attachment fixed to the side of the open cockpit to steady the camera. Whole areas of Aberdeen in this picture have now disappeared. Note the cluster of houses which was Old Torry and the long gone shipyard close by on the south of the harbour. Steam trawlers lie at anchor in the centre channel. The picture is undated but Brian Harwood of Northfield, Aberdeen, noticed the UAS marking on the nose of the Tiger Moth denoting the University Air Squadron which was formed in January 1941. Brian, who researched the military history of RAF Dyce, says that in 1943 Aberdeen University had to share an aircraft with the Edinburgh University Air Squadron until they received their own Tiger Moths in 1944/45.

Families of the Battery

These next three pictures from Leonard Pelman were taken in 1935. Although no captions survive I believe they show a time when Aberdeen's housing problems forced families to stay in the Torry Point Battery. Veterans remember the Battery being used by the military in the 1920s but there seems to have been a break before World War Two. Certainly the Battery housed families after the war when there was a desperate shortage of houses. According to newspapers of the time 19 families were housed at Torry Battery from early 1945 until 1953 when the housing situation improved. There were nine one-apartment homes, with two-apartment and three-apartment houses as well.

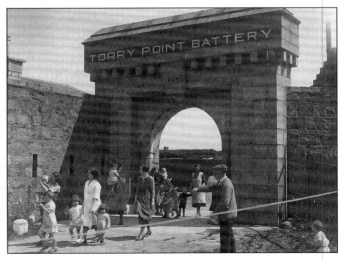

A warm spell of weather in the early Thirties brought the crowds out. Here the River Dee can be seen with many small craft on the water. Perhaps that's what attracted the crowds seen strolling along beside the river.

An Aberdeen boat race with two sets of rowers and their coxes at the Victoria Bridge in the 1930s. Note the posts on the bridge carrying wires for the Torry trams and the the high harbour cranes which can be seen beyond the bridge.

The hurdy-gurdy man entertains children in Urquhart Road in the 1930s.

A royal guard of honour at Ballater Station. A cameraman films the scene from the top of a motor vehicle.

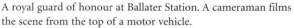

Leisure

A small girl is one of the few people to be seen on Aberdeen's historic beach promenade on this bracing day in April 1951.

Revellers at the Beach Ballroom in Aberdeen. It's just after the war and everyone's determined to enjoy themselves despite the austerity years that lie ahead. This picture from Margaret Masson of Summerhill, Aberdeen, shows the popularity of the Lambeth Walk.

Magnificent men and women on their magnificent machines at Bon Accord Street, Aberdeen around 1912. The picture came from Kitty Strachan of Guthrie, by Forfar. Her father is fourth from the right with her mother in the sidecar at this souvenir motor cycle club rally picture.

Smile for the camera. This fine Edwardian group is farmer Willie Ross and his grandchildren. It was probably taken in 1910. Once a year Willie, who farmed at Monymusk loaded his grandchildren on to horses and carts and took them to Aberdeen Beach. On the extreme right is John Ross who became mine host at the City Bar. Picture courtesy of Moira Timmerman of Milltimber.

A great golfer is about to strike the golf ball at the opening of Hazlehead Golf Course. On the tee is Dr William Tweddell who has just been crowned British Amateur champion. Dr Tweddell studied medicine at Aberdeen University. At one stage he played off a handicap of plus 3. Waiting his turn on the left is the legendary J. H. Taylor who was Open champion five times. Along with Harry Vardon and James Braid he was part of the great golfing triumvirate of his day. A crowd of 6,000 followed the first round at Hazlehead on 2 July 1927. Both golfers equalled the course bogey of 76. The picture is courtesy of noted amateur golfer Sandy Pirie who followed in his father's footsteps and became head greenkeeper at Hazlehead before entering the licensed trade.

A happy picture from the days when Woolworths sold nothing priced over 6d (2½p). Mrs J. Reid of Aberdeen, who handed in the picture, is standing at the back on the left of the bus. The year is 1947 and it's the first bus outing for the St Nicholas Street branch workers.

They're off! The moment when racing started at Aberdeen's new Greyhound Stadium on 7 June 1933. For 36 years Aberdonians 'went to the dogs' with the post war years seeing its popularity as a spectator sport second only to football. As well as the crowds within the stadium there was another group keeping an eye on the races from the aptly-named Misers' Hilly above the track. In those glory years the dogs attracted a rich collection of characters. Norman Herd of Garthdee, Aberdeen, who clerked for his brother Doug at the track, recalls bookmakers Mac Davidson, Bobby Morrison and Jim Rennie, known to all as Swifty. There was also the colourful punters – the Twinnies, Pooches and Chocolate Beattie.

The original Frankie and the Strollers group. This picture is from 1962 and was taken at the Beehive club in Northfield. The line-up is Bill Spiers, bass; George Barker, rhythm guitar, Bill Gauld, drums; Denny Greig, lead guitar, Julie Barker and singer Frank Milne. Sometimes known as Frankie, Julie and the Strollers. Today George Barker and his sister Julie do cabaret work in Darwin, Australia. Vocalist Frankie Milne and Bill Spiers play as a duo under the name of Swingshift.

Tommy Dene and The Tremors, pictured in August 1963.

The Quantrells in their 1967 pop gear. This was the final line-up of the well-known North-East group which played its last gig at the Beach Ballroom on 9 September 1967. In this picture are Raymond Ross, Gus McLellan, Bryson Kemp, Les Cumming and Bill Spratt. Bryson still has contracts from the Sixties which show the fee for a support gig at the Palace and Beach was £7 10s for a full night.

The fans at a 1966 beat group festival at the YMCA in Aberdeen. The group playing was the Beathovens. The girls are, from second left, Laraine Archibald (Watson) who sang with the Quantrells, Kathleen Davidson and Caroline Shand.

Taking time out to sketch one of Aberdeen's landmarks in the Sixties – the Well of Spa which was then set into the wall of Woolmanhill Hospital in Spa Street but which is now round the corner at Skene Street.

The Carcone family outside the White Rose fish restaurant at 12 Causewayend, Aberdeen, in the 1960s. This picture created a great response from readers who had many happy memories of the friendly family and their cafe which was noted for its fish and chips and ice cream. It was a magnet for members of the nearby Lads' Club. One of those boys was John McDonald of Balmedie who fondly remembers Joe Carcone, Lena, Vincent and Mary.

The Dee Club held annual 'Aquatic Sports' events near the Victoria Bridge in the 1930s. Mr R. Sanderson, general secretary of the present day swimming club, explained that the galas were in aid of the Aberdeen Hospitals Fund. The 1936 event, which is pictured, drew 15,000 spectators to the banks of the River Dee. The main event was a 220-yard race for the Smith Challenge Shield which was retained by James Main. There was a high diving exhibition from a platform on the Victoria Bridge and a demonstration of life saving techniques. The gala raised £16 11s 2d for Aberdeen hospitals. Mrs Emily McLean remembers taking part in some of the events with her husband Bill. She says: "We swam to the boathouse where we were given a hot pie and Oxo. Nothing ever tasted quite like that pie and Oxo which warmed us up."

A large crowd looks on at Central Park, Aberdeen, in 1958 as Banks o' Dee forward McCrae has a shot blocked by Stroud the Hall Russell keeper. The two junior football teams are contesting the final of the coveted Duthie Cup.

Last race meeting. A big turn-out in September 1928 for the final horse races at Seaton, Aberdeen.

Picnic time at the Bay of Nigg in the early 1930s. It is the extended family of Aberdeen fish merchant George Robertson. Picture courtesy of Bill Morrice who is George Robertson's grandson.

The Linksfield School football team of 1943 with the Aberdeen School Shield which they won in a final at Pittodrie. It was the second year running they had won the shield. Gordon Bathgate (third left, back row) recalls they were coached by the school janitor, a Mr Bisset. Gordon says: "What a great feeling it was to run on to Pittodrie Park, especially as we played most of our matches at Nelson Street playing fields which did not have a blade of grass." Linksfield contested the final for the shield the following year, losing out to Causewayend School.

The beauty of Marchmont Gardens, Rubislaw Den South, Aberdeen, is admired by visitors in 1955 when the remarkable private gardens were opened in aid of a Boys' Brigade appeal.

Conjuring up a galloping horse for radio listeners with two coconut shells. Melville Dinwoodie is demonstrating the special sound effect at the BBC's Beechgrove House, Aberdeen, in 1948.

The trek cart which the 11th Scout Troop used in pre-war days to get their tents and other equipment to Templar's Park at Maryculter. Although he didn't recognise any of the Scouts, Gordon Bissett remembered the trek cart. Gordon, former Picture Editor of the *Evening Express* explained that the Scouts devised a way of pulling the cart with two cyclists at the front and two outriders controlling the vehicle on downhill sections and helping to push when hills were encountered. Gordon says: "One day the low-slung cart was covered with a tarpaulin and could pass for a gun carriage on a dull morning. When we encountered two policemen, instead of telling us off one solemnly removed his helmet and placed it over his chest in mock respect."

Opening day. A souvenir picture from 9 May 1914 when Sir Alexander Lyon opened the new green of the Northern Bowling Club, Orchard Road, Aberdeen, by throwing a silver jack. Sir Alexander was at that time Lord Provost. He made a big impression on the city playing a leading role in laying out the Westburn and Victoria parks as well as Union Terrace Gardens.

The cinema organists were local personalities from pre-war years right through to the Fifties. In Aberdeen Bobby Pagan (left), who usually wore a kilt, and George Blackmore (above) were two of the favourites. Mr R. J. Nicol of Ferryhill, Aberdeen, listed the musicians by cinema. Astoria: Harold Titherington, Charles Saxby, Bobby Pagan, Norman Whitehead, George Blackmore. The Capitol: Harold Coombs and F. Rowland Tims.

Children's entertainment at Aberdeen Beach in 1972 with a sack race being keenly contested on the sands.

Getting in the swim at Quarryhill Primary School, Aberdeen, in 1971 thanks to the determination of head teacher Lawrence Haywood. Eric Hendrie, education convener at the time, is pictured blowing a whistle as the first pupils try out the new pool. He recalls that Mr Haywood drove him to Laurencekirk to see a similar self-contained pool to persuade him it was right for Quarryhill.

Happy to be flying off. Aberdeen sunseekers prepare to leave the wind and rain at Aberdeen Airport for the first direct commercial flight from the city to Palma, Majorca, in 1973. The 94-seat Caravelle jet was fully booked for the flight.

Smiling through. A family on Aberdeen Beach in the 1950s refuses to abandon their day on the sands… despite the weather.

Happy summer days at the Lynn Park Tea Gardens near Aberdeen in 1938. Bill Jamieson (pictured right on the swings) contributed this picture of a popular leisure spot for Aberdonians near the Mill Inn on the South Deeside Road. George Keith of Newtonhill remembered that there were tennis courts and a small boating pool as well as the tea rooms. George and his friends, who were shop assistants in Aberdeen, used to catch the Strachan's bus to take them to the gardens on their Wednesday half-day off.

Another view of the Lynn Park courtesy of Albert J. Moir of Peterculter who says this picture was taken around 1925 and that the park closed in 1939 and the buildings were pulled down after the war.

Work

The men of granite line up for a picture in 1937. Stan McKenzie of Beechwood Road, Aberdeen, submitted this picture and pointed out the men all lived in the Orchard Street and Old Aberdeen area. This vital part of the city's commercial past could be a harsh job. John R. Watt of Linksfield Place said the photograph was taken at the former Gibbs Excelsior Granite Works on Linksfield Road. Mr Watt's father, also John, is pictured middle row, fourth left. John senior's brother and his father before him worked as stonemasons and lettercutters. John R. Watt remembers that the men had little or no protection from granite dust and dampness resulting in chest infections. All letter cutting was done by hand with hammer and chisel.

A souvenir picture from 1939 of the workforce at the Aberdeen engineering firm George Cassie and Son. The firm specialised in granite working machinery. The picture came from George Milne of Kincorth, Aberdeen (the young chap centre of second row). Frank Cassie, the son of the founder, is pictured extreme left in hat. In front of him on the second row is Pat Smith the works foreman.

A picture of one of Aberdeen's most influential entrepreneurs from the days when a visit from the photographer was obviously a serious business. On the extreme left is the young James Forrest Donald, founder of the city's entertainment dynasty. The picture was taken at the north side of the Castlegate and reflects several of J. F. Donald's interests. The Highland dancer John Findlay (second left) is the father of William Findlay of Mastrick who provided this picture. John says the dancer Jeannie Hendry (front, second right) later ran her own dancing school. The cycling theme is probably explained by J. F. Donald's reputation as an excellent cyclist. William Findlay says the large gentleman in the centre of the

picture was known as The Fat Boy. He apparently cycled around Aberdeen demonstrating the robustness of Cleveland Cycles. J. F. Donald bought the Gondolier Dance Hall in North Silver Street in 1902, the base for his dance academy. His business took in the Cinema House. The West End Cinema, later to become The Playhouse, was also acquired. The firm grew steadily for 30 years as it fed the public's considerable appetite for the silver screen. At one time the Donald family owned 15 cinemas. J. F. Donald bought His Majesty's Theatre in 1933. He died in 1934 aged 64. We reckon the picture shows J. F. when he was aged about 24.

A moment from one of the annual dinner dances of the Donald family entertainment empire at the Douglas Hotel, Market Street, in the 1950s. Mrs Evelyn Reid (née Leys), an usherette at the Majestic cinema from 1948 to 1957, is receiving a prize of a box of knives from Mrs Herbert Donald. Evelyn looks back on her days at the Majestic with great affection.

A celebration picture at the opening of the art deco Carron Restaurant in Stonehaven in June 1937. This picture came from Mrs Rachel Yorston of Mannofield, Aberdeen, whose late father Victor Lorimer is in the third row from the front, second right. The headline-grabbing building on Cameron Street became the focal point for Stonehaven's social life. It was part of a Northern Co-operative Society development. The building closed to the public in 1968 and fell into disrepair, but the B-listed building has never been short of restoration plans.

Two generations of workers at Hamilton Bros, the Buckie ship repair company. They worked on boilers and engines for steam trawlers and also did a lot of work for distilleries. The company prospered until the fishing fleet declined. The 1952 (above) picture was taken at a retirement presentation for a blacksmith.

The rush home at the end of the working day at Aberdeen's Hall Russell shipbuilding yard in the 1950s.

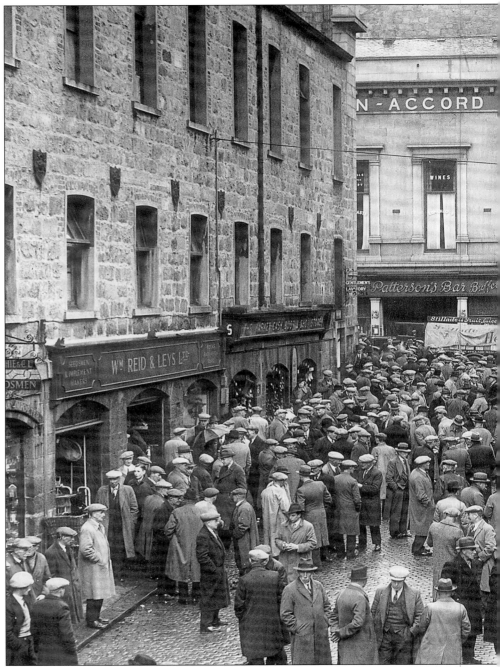

One of the popular meeting places when country came to town on market day. This is Hadden Street, Aberdeen, in the 1930s. The seed merchant shops in the area were the magnet for the farmers.

The flag-bedecked St Rognvald ferry is escorted to the fitting-out dock after being launched from the Alexander Hall yard in Aberdeen, 1954.

Cooper James Rae outside the John Robertson cooperage in Hanover Lane, Aberdeen, in 1937. The young lads taking a wary look at the barrel makers' handiwork for the distilleries are George Brands, David Murray and Seaton Brands who all lived in Hanover Lane, a lively little community in those days. The picture came from Mrs Grace Ross of Torry, sister of the late James Rae.

In its hey day the village of Kemnay supported three bakery firms which were all next to one another in the same street. Duncan Downie of Kemnay wrote saying that in 1863 George Gellie, one of the early entrepreneurs in the village took a lease of a portion of ground across the road from the railway station. He built a tenement and a shop alongside, in the property now occupied by The Laird's Throat bar and restaurant. John MacDonald, a baker, leased this shop.

When Leslie Adam, another early entrepreneur who dealt in coal, cattle feed and other commodities, built the property across the lane in 1877 – that shown in our 1920s photograph – John MacDonald moved into the shop.

In time his son-in-law William Snowie took over the business. He was followed by George McKay who was in turn followed by Thomas Milne. The last baker to occupy the premises was A. & S. Taylor. Norman Lawrence used it as a store for a number of years. Isaac Wright, also a baker, followed John MacDonald in Gellie's building. The building had several uses before it was opened as a public bar in the early 1950s by John Gibb who named it Gushet Neuk after the North-East literary classic.

The man on the left of the picture is James Rainnie. Of local stock he worked as a vanman all his life, almost to his death in 1965 aged 81. One of his well-known traits as he travelled the countryside was his driving speed. I am told that even in the 1960s he rarely exceeded 20mph. The figure by his side is his son Sandy who was born around 1917-18. Sandy, it is understood, now lives in Aberdeen.

In 1901 George B. Adams took a lease of the land next to Leslie Adam and built a shop and a house. Known as Pie Dod, Adams had moved from a shop in Thorpeville, further up the village, but he did not reign long in Station Road as the lease was taken over by Alexander Henry in 1906. The property was run as the Temperance Hotel for a good number of years and the Henry's baked enough goods to serve those using the hotel, getting yeast from the Snowie's up the road. Eventually it became a bakery with the hall being used as the bakehouse. It closed as a bakery in 1969 and has seen various uses since.

Women in the burling room at Crombie Mills, Grandholm, in 1965. The long-established firm produced overcoats for soldiers from the Napoleonic wars to World War Two and beyond. Crombie cloth also clothed Russian soldiers and the nation's leaders alike. At one time 700 people were employed at the mill. Now the site of the huge factory is being turned into a housing development.

An aerial picture of the huge site covered by the J. J. Crombie company in its days as a world renowned producer of fine cloth.

The hard back-straining work of tattie picking in the 1950s. Before machinery took over this work children had short "tattie holidays" from school to work in the fields – a tradition which continued long beyond the need for a concerted effort to harvest the potato drills.

Fishermen at work in their souwesters on the trawler Strathcoe in October 1958. The boat is a typical Smokie Joe, or coal burner, one of a huge fishing fleet which sailed out of Aberdeen. Sadly five months after this picture was taken the Strathcoe sank off Orkney. Fortunately all hands were saved by the Longhope Lifeboat in a gale. Strathcoe crewman Ian Scott of Premnay, who provided this picture, sailed for many more years on other boats and in the Merchant Marine service.

The staff of the Woodside Works – or more popularly The Rugger – gather around the oldest employee Lizzie Scofield as she accepts a good housekeeping trophy on behalf of the workers. On the left is J. T. Mackie, manager of the works which were part of Stoneywood Mills. They processed raw materials like rags, preparing them for paper making. The Rugger closed in the early 60s. This picture came from Godfrey Mackie, of Great Northern Road, Aberdeen, the son of J. T. Mackie, who also worked at the Woodside Works and met his wife there.

The mercy men. A group picture taken of the men of Aberdeen's St Andrew's Ambulance Service in the 1950s before they moved from Fetter Garage at the foot of Kintore Place to their new premises in Ashgrove Road West. In those days the ambulances were brown with black fenders. Then they were blue for a time before the present white colour was adopted. This picture comes from William Mennie of Heathryfold, Aberdeen. His late father, also William, is third right, back row.

The ambulance depot at Ashgrove Road West just after it was opened in the 1950s. The depot cost £25,000 and housed 12 ambulances. The distinctive barrel-vaulted roof allowed the interior to be free of pillars.

Aberdeen harbour in the 1900s showing the tracer horses at the foot of Market Street. In those days carters' horses needed help when heavy loads were hauled up the slope of Market Street. That's when teams of the tracer horses were used to supply extra pulling power to get the loads up to Union Street.

The once famous Fidler's Well in Guild Street, Aberdeen. Its waters were used to slake the thirst of many a hard working horse. The well, erected in 1857 by a coal broker named Alexander Fidler, was dedicated to William Guild the 17th-century minister whose name was given to Guild Street. Alexander Fidler died in 1885 and his well was still in place in 1957.

An atmospheric picture of Aberdeen Harbour in February 1956, showing the trawler *Gava* which ran aground in the navigation channel as she set out for the fishing grounds.

The ocean-going tug *Tusker* is launched at the Footdee yard of Alexander Hall and Co in 1956 with some of the proud workers aboard.

In time of war many of the most significant changes came to our society. This picture is captioned: 'Aberdeen's female car conductors – full staff, June 19, 1915'. It shows the women who took over jobs left by the men fighting World War One. Before the necessities of war dictated otherwise this would not have been considered a suitable job for women in the Edwardian society.

Clippies on parade at Aberdeen's Duthie Park in 1948. These smart W. Alexander & Sons conductresses, complete with their clipping machines, were seen as a good model for the rest of the country. The northern area of Alexander's stretched from Dundee to Elgin and their conductresses had a reputation for being particularly well turned out. The picture is courtesy of James Tweedie, an assistant traffic manager at the Gairn Terrace depot at the time the picture was taken.

The coopers of John Robertson and Sons pose for a picture in 1939. The firm used to turn out barrels from premises in Aberdeen's Hanover Lane.

The milkman and milkboys of Torry in the 1920s. The horse-drawn cart was from South Kirkhill dairy farm on St Fittick's Road. The boys collected flagons from the houses and got them filled with fresh milk from churns on the cart. After this picture was published in the *Evening Express* Alistair Milne of Redmoss wrote to say the picture shows his father John (left), farmer Corbett and the other boy is John Cowe. Alistair's father was born in 1909 and died in 1996. The milkboy grew up to spend 42 years in the Aberdeen trawl fishing industry. John Milne served on minesweepers during World War Two.

The Kennerty milkman doing his rounds in the West End of Aberdeen in 1961. The milkman was recognised by Aberdeen councillor Len Ironside as his uncle John Cumming. Len recalls helping his uncle on Saturdays and admiring the way John could lift six full cases of milk at once. He adds: "Uncle John was most fussy about his milk boys. He insisted they wear a collar and tie and that their shoes were brushed up to a highly polished shine. He would not have anyone leaving milk at the door of his customers looking scruffy."

Ready to serve. The men of William Davidson, wholesale druggists, of Palmerston Road, Aberdeen, in the 1920s when the firm founded in 1866 was flourishing as an independent company. Founder William Davidson was a druggist's apprentice from New Deer. In 1925 the Palmerston Road premises were gutted by a disastrous fire made worse by the chemicals stored there. The company found temporary accommodation to continue trading, returning later to Palmerston Road where it remained until 1970. The firm was taken over by a national pharmaceuticals concern in 1991.

Aberdeen fisher lassies and lads at the Torry premises of Direct Fish Supply in the 1950s.

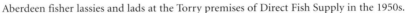

Meet the bannermen. These are the men of housebuilder J. Bisset after they erected one of a series of banners which became a focal point of Aberdeen's home front effort during World War Two. Sandy Reid (third left), who worked on three such banners for the front of the Music Hall, provided the picture of the men. The banners went up for money-raising weeks between 1942 and 1944 which always culminated with a parade down Union Street. Mr Reid of Great Southern Road said a local artist spent weeks painting the posters in full colour.

One of the huge banners produced for the money-raising campaigns. This one was for the Wings for Victory Week in June 1943. It was just one of a series of campaigns which raised millions of pounds for the war effort.

Aberdeen Memories: A Hidden Archive Uncovered

Aberdeen Harbour Board's collection of thousands of glass plate negatives from the 1880s to 1930s are a remarkable record of the city's gateway to the world. Taken by engineers at a time of great growth at the harbour they are now a unique record of that age. As this is written the collection is being printed and loaded on to an Internet web site created and maintained by the University of Aberdeen. It can be viewed at www.abdn.ac.uk/library/harbour.

Work

In the picture below ships are loaded up at Blaikies Quay in 1908. In the foreground is the steam cargo ship *Ballochbuie* and in the background the unusual shape of HMS *Clyde*. At the bottom right is a toll bothy.

A view of the harbour in 1922 showing the bucket dredger *Dragon*, a steam paddle tug and, in the distance, a line of horse-drawn carts crossing St Clements Bridge.

Work under way at Aberdeen Harbour in 1909 on the giant shear legs which were to be used for lifting heavy cargoes for many decades.

Thirteen lifeboatmen stand proudly aboard their lifeboat on Commercial Quay in 1933 ready to take part in a procession. Below the lifeboat a cheeky boy sneaks into the picture.

The steam bucket dredger *Sea Worker* in action at the Torry side of the harbour in 1914 with the hopper barge *Slogan* lying alongside. In the foreground a clinker-built cobble is manoeuvred over towards the workings.

A ferry boat crossing Aberdeen Harbour heading for Albert Quay. The boat is pulled by a winch with a wire stretched between the two landing stages. The five men and a boy in the boat are leaving the graving dock stage. This picture would have been taken before 1909.

Steam tugs at the Victoria Dock entrance including the paddle vessels *John McConnachie* and the *Granite City*, with Aberdeen Harbour's own *John Graham* tug in the foreground. A sign for the Fittie Bar can be seen to the left in this picture from around 1910.

Aberdeen Harbour Pontoon Dock operators pose proudly for the camera with a steam cargo vessel on the Pontoon in 1910.

Victoria Dock gate house around the time of its opening in 1897. Note the handcart being pushed across the bridge.

Harbour workers in a small boat pull alongside Aberdeen Harbour's *John Graham* tug in the Victoria Dock around 1910.

The well-stocked Culter branch of the Northern Co-operative Society around 1928. This picture came from Mrs Margaret Massie and Mrs Frances Calder of Aberdeen whose father Frank Garden is second from the right behind the counter. Mr Garden went on to be manager of the Co-op at Banchory. He died aged 53. The young man (third left) Donald Quirie died during World War Two as did George Still (behind chair) who served with the RAF.

One of Aberdeen's most remarkable institutions is the Shore Porters' Society. The company's claim to have been 'established in 1498' is certainly modest. The general carriers and removal contractors were in operation much earlier than the 15th century but their first mention on a charter is dated 22nd of June 1498.

The Society's remarkable history is recorded by George Gordon in a book for the 500th anniversary. It has since been updated and it will probably need many more revisions as the Society continues to thrive into the 21st century.

Before the hearse was invented the Shore Porters carried out the sombre act of carrying coffins. This picture shows a funeral party in the early 1900s. In Victorian and Edwardian times they were much sought after to add dignity to such occasions. The tall carriers wore black jackets with coat tails and distinctive round bonnets. By the start of World War Two the motor hearse had almost completely replaced this custom.

Members of the Shore Porters' Society of Aberdeen pictured at their Shore Lane premises in 1903.

Workers at the Shore Porters' Society Cotton Street stables in 1903.

One of Aberdeen's best loved companies of the 19th and 20th century was John E. Esslemont. Set up in 1864 it started in tiny premises as a retail grocery and confectionery shop. But the attractiveness of their products and the sweet tooth of the Aberdeen public soon ensured the firm was famed far and wide as a sweetie shop. For more than a century it thrived and grew. In 1964 it was a tea blending and packeting house for shopkeepers throughout Scotland. It was also a wholesale hardware business, a factory turning out tons of sweets a week and a wholesale confectionery business. And it was a family grocer's shop on King Street, not far from the original premises – but six times the size.

A night out for the staff of John E. Esslemont with the founder pictured centre with beard.

A mouth-watering consignment of tons of chocolate and confectionery from Needlers arrives at John E. Esslemont's premises in 1911 with wide-eyed children looking on. Just over a year later the firm took delivery of a record-breaking 46 tons of chocolate and confectionery. The consignment from Glasgow required 22 horse lorries which paraded down Aberdeen's Union Street.

Pictures from a collection held by Alan Esslemont of Aberdeen.

Some of the John E. Esslemont girls who helped bring the finest sweets and confectionery to Aberdeen folk.

The staff and owners of John E. Esslemont outside their fine King Street premises as the firm began to expand.

A line-up of proud Post Office Telegraph messenger boys with their brand new bikes. No more push bikes for these 17-year-olds astride their green BSA Bantams. Chief mechanic Albert Henderson is looking on in this picture taken in March 1950. The picture came courtesy of John Irvine, second right, and Len Freund, fourth left. John recalled: "The Bantams got up to 56mph flat out downhill with a following wind." In the heyday of the telegram more than 1,000 would be delivered a day. John added that the *Evening Express* and *Press and Journal* had the heaviest deliveries followed by the fish trade with its telegram orders. "A wedding wasn't a wedding without a telegram," said John. The Inland Telegram Service ended in October 1982, a victim of rising costs and new modes of communication.

Fred Lenkie, the doorman at the General Post Office headquarters on Crown Street, Aberdeen, congratulates three of the messenger boys as they sit astride their new bikes. They are (from left) Len Freund, A. Reid and K. Somers. Picture courtesy of Len Freund.

Famous Faces & Places

Ferry Bell feeds swans beside her boat at Blairs, near Aberdeen. Bella (Isabel) Main, known to all as Ferry Bell, ran the ferry across the River Dee and also a popular tearoom where she sold tea and home baking to visitors. Before Bell retired and the ferry on Lower Deeside stopped operating, the Blairs Ferry was a popular meeting place for locals, Aberdeen visitors and, particularly, cycling clubs. Even as Bell grew older she would continue to take people across the stretch of water. Bell was the last ferry operator on the Dee, continuing until the early 1960s. Born in 1896 she died in 1989.

Another of the Dee's ferrywomen was Boatie Maggie at Peterculter. Here she can be seen with a client in the 1920s. Albert Moir of Peterculter, who provided this picture, said Boatie Maggie rowed from the south bank of the Dee to the shore beside the churchyard at Peterculter. Albert remembers Maggie's surname was Irvine and she continued her ferrying service until the Thirties.

An unexpected side of the famous Aberdeen-born footballer Denis Law is shown in this picture from the summer of 1958. Denis, who was playing for Bill Shankly's Huddersfield at the time was on a camping holiday in Blackpool with three of his chums. That week the rock and roll star Tommy Steele was playing at the Blackpool Tower and the 18-year-old Denis kept getting mistaken for him and asked for his autograph. Hebbie Cheyne of Mastrick, Aberdeen, who provided this picture, recalls that the mistaken identity prompted Denis to pose like a rock star of the time when they returned to their campsite. Hebbie remembers that the friends made the holiday trip in a Ford Prefect with dodgy suspension.

A familiar looking face at Aberdeen Joint Station in 1938. The man with the distinctive Kennedy features is Joseph, father of Jack, Bobby and Edward, and founder of the American political dynasty. In 1938 he was the US Ambassador to Britain. Meeting him is Bishop Deane, the Episcopalian Bishop of Aberdeen and Orkney. They went on to Bishops Court, 29 Albyn Place. The Bishop lived there until 1943. After that the house was run as a hotel and then became the Railway Club until it closed down a few years ago.

The Dancers of Don, a well-known group of expert country dancers from the Thirties. They were organised by Elizabeth Forbes-Sempill (front centre) from 1933. In 1937 they danced at the great Paris Exhibition. This picture comes courtesy of Dael Ogilvie of Peterculter who pointed out that Elizabeth Forbes-Sempill who is in this group re-registered her birth as Ewan in 1952 and married his former housekeeper. Sir Ewan Forbes became the 11th Baronet of Craigievar and died aged 79 in 1991.

A very special moment for these girls of Hilton School choir as they proudly display the Innes Rosebowl they have just won at the Aberdeen Music Festival in 1957. The picture came from Mrs Marion Duncan (second girl from the left, front row) who said the choir sang their hearts out competing against choirs from the whole of north Scotland. Their teacher was Helen Currie who says: "I remember the occasion very clearly when they, resplendent in white blouses, navy skirts and school ties, gave a wonderful performance." She adds that the cup is still competed for.

These raffle prizes at the Snow Ball don't look very enticing because it's the post-war austerity years. Note that one of the prizes is a basket of eggs. The charity-raising event began in 1945 organised by the League of Pity, a junior branch of the Royal Scottish Society for the Prevention of Cruelty to Children. In 1946 the Snow Ball raised a remarkable £1,200 when the main guests were soldiers newly returned from the war and prison camps. Rationing meant even the hall decorations were sparse. The Snow Ball remains a big Aberdeen social occasion to this day – and an impressive contributor to the charity Children 1st.

The Aberdeen entertainer famous as 'the smiling face of radio'. George Elrick – known as Mrs Elrick's wee son George – is seen here with the US singer Connie Francis at a 1960 Variety Club event at The Dorchester Hotel in London for men and women who had sold more than one million records. George was one of a family of nine who lived in a tenement in Cotton Street. But George's ability as a drummer set him on a remarkable journey… band leader, personality, radio star. His long career and charming personality made him the friend of many of the world's most famous people. George died in 1999 aged 95.

The winners of a beauty competition the *Evening Express* ran in 1954 mix with the stars. Kay McGowan (left) and Maida Hector won a trip to Elstree Studios, London, in the contest to mark the opening of Aberdeen's Regal Cinema on Union Street. Kay says they were treated to a dinner at Aberdeen's Station Hotel with Richard Todd (above) who opened the Regal. The next day the girls flew to Elstree where they met Peter Finch and the legendary Errol Flynn (left) who was making one of his swashbuckling movies. "The competition was a real thrill for us," says Kay of Cattofield Place. "Meeting the stars, flying for the first time and staying at the wonderful Grosvenor House Hotel."

Expectant looks on the faces of this crowd at Ballater waiting for the royal family to arrive in 1948. On the left with the Box Brownie is Bill Morrice who handed in the picture.

The illusionist Walford Brodie, right, with his friend Aberdeen businessman Fred Webster. Edwin Webster of Aberdeen provided this picture. He says his late father considered the famous Thirties showman an exceptional magician with many baffling tricks.

An encore by first-prize winner William Miller of Aberdeen at a talent contest at the Beach in July 1952. On the right is Leslie Thorpe, leader of the Beach Ballroom band, who judged the contest.

Aberdeen Beach Ballroom resident band leader Leslie Thorpe pictured in 1958 with saxophonist W. Robinson, at that time the only remaining member of the band which first struck up at the popular dance venue a decade before.

Aberdeen's 'Mr Music' at the Beach Ballroom for a decade was Leslie Thorpe seen here conducting his band. This picture was taken in 1958.

The University of Aberdeen Debater celebrated 150 years of free speech in October 1998. Our picture is from the sedate debating society committee of 1951-52. But by the mid Sixties times had changed. Dr J. P. Reid of Burns Road, Aberdeen, wrote: 'When I came up in 1964 it was all very traditional. Formal academic dress for the committee, white tie and tails. There was quite a change in 1965 when the president, George Muir, wore sandals and a "sloppy joe" under his gown. Debating topics became more serious. Politicians were invited. Donald Dewar with his reputation for being the fastest talking MP, Teddy Taylor, Judith Hart and many others. We also had Archie Hinds the great escaper, but our best catch was J. K. Galbraith the Harvard professor.' Dr Reid was Debater vice-president to Tom Snow during the hotly-contested Rectorial contest of 1966-67. This reached a dramatic conclusion during the debate in the Mitchell Hall: "Tom wanted to speak and stood down from the chair passing command to me," says Dr Reid. "Tom started speaking and deliberately wouldn't stop. The rabble became more and more incensed and just before a real riot broke out I remembered the time-honoured phrase and bellowed into the microphone: 'Mr Snow I can no longer afford you the protection of the chair.'" Whereupon a dozen hotheads rushed forward, grabbed Tom, and carried him horizontally out of the building while he continued his speech complete with waving arms. The whole 'show' closed in happy uproar."

In 1957 singing stars seemed a lot more approachable than they do today. Can you imagine one of the present-day idols treating their fans to a tea party? But that's exactly what happened when Frankie Vaughan came to town. Eileen Stephen still remembers that day when she met her hero. She says: "As a member of Rosemount Youth Club I was lucky enough to be picked to meet Frankie Vaughan at the Caledonian Hotel. On arrival we were all issued with a name tag before being ushered into the function room. When the big star arrived we were all under his spell immediately. He talked to us all individually and during the party I asked if he would sing for us. He sang *When I Fall In Love*. Halfway through the song he stood up and started singing just to me. Then he kissed me on the forehead and placed me back in my seat in a trance. The picture appeared in the *Evening Express* the next day." The picture above shows Frankie signing his autograph for Eileen.

The staff at the Rothes estate of the Grant family of whisky fame in 1901. Fourth from the left in the back row is Leo Freund, the grandfather of Len Freund of Aberdeen who provided the picture. Leo's story is a fascinating one. As a young man in Homburg, Germany, he and a friend tossed a coin to decide where they would go to make their way in life – London or Paris. London won and soon Leo had a job there as a waiter. From there he moved to the prestigious North British Hotel in Edinburgh where he caught the eye of the Grant family and was offered a job in Rothes as butler. He met his wife Ann in Rothes but in 1909 Leo moved to the United States to further his career. After a few years he had established himself there and had a good job and house for his family to go to. But fate intervened with the sinking of the *Titanic* in 1912. Although they were packed and ready to go to the US Ann refused point blank to sail the Atlantic. Leo returned to Britain and a job in the Borders where he worked until the outbreak of World War One. Because he was German Leo was interned in the Isle of Man despite efforts by the Grant family on his behalf. Even his wife Ann, then back staying in Rothes, had to report to the police in Rothes once a week. At the end of the war Leo was deported back to Germany and his wife and three children stayed in Britain. Ann died in 1920 having never seen her husband again. Len's father Leonard didn't see his father until 1927

when he was a teenager. He met Leo again in 1938 before World War Two when there was another lengthy break in contact until 1951 before the two branches of the family met again. Leo died in 1962 aged 83. Also in the 1901 picture is a young man Len understands was named Biewa. He was brought to Rothes from West Africa. Leo taught him English. Biewa stayed in the area for the rest of his life and became an avid football supporter.

The famous conductor Sir Thomas Beecham at a 1930s concert in the North-East.

The people of Aberdeen cheer their victorious war leader Winston Churchill as he drives to the Music Hall to be made a Freeman of the city on 27 April 1946. Alongside Churchill is Lord Provost Sir Thomas Mitchell.

Aberdeen's new Freeman walks up Union Street with his wife Clementine and daughter Mary in April 1946. Winston Churchill is wearing the ceremonial Burgess Ticket tied to his hat.

Aberdeen aviation pioneer Captain Ernest Fresson beside one of his Monospar planes. In 1934 he inaugurated one of the city's first scheduled flights using an airstrip at Seaton. His great rival in the air business in Aberdeen was Gandar Dower.

The founding father of Dyce airport, Gandar Dower, spreads his political message for the 1945 General Election. He pioneered scheduled air services to Edinburgh, Glasgow and Shetland in 1934. By 1937 he even had an air link with Norway.

Members of the capacity audience at the Rolling Stones concert in the Capitol, Aberdeen, in 1982 show their appreciation. Some of them had paid more than £100 a ticket to see their idols who had last appeared in Aberdeen 17 years earlier.

Two travelling people by the side of a road in Deeside in 1954. A pram serves as a handcart for the couple and the woman enjoys her pipe as they rest.

Moment of no return during parachute training in Aberdeen.

Study in devotion during a Bay City Rollers concert in Aberdeen at the height of their fame.

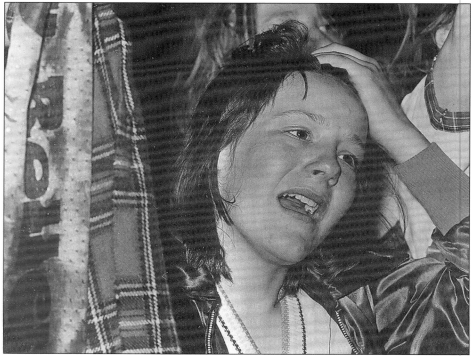

A sheep grabs some hay during a harsh North-East winter as the resourceful farmer straps on his skis.

The Queen pauses for a moment while the Duke of Edinburgh discusses navigation details during a visit to a ship in Aberdeen in 1977.

Transport

Starting out. The 15-year-old Albert More (right) stands beside the van he went on to drive the next year. The driver standing beside young Albert in this picture from the 1920s is Adam Gerrie. Adam will be remembered by many as the man who ran the Bridge of Dee Post Office on Aberdeen's Holburn Street.

Albert More pictured aged 94 years in 1999.

Slowly …steadily, the former Aberdeen County Council steam-driven road roller makes its way through Inverurie en route from Port Elphinstone to Harlaw Road in March 1977.

November 1955 and locals turn out to wave goodbye to the last tram to Woodside. Three years later, the very last tram of all rattled over the city's cobbled streets.

A grand gathering of bedecked trams at Queen's Cross on the Golden Jubilee of the Aberdeen tram system in 1924. The picture came into the possession of John Clark and family of Kincorth when John's son Steven noticed the set of pictures at an antique fair and realised they featured a relative. Mr Clark's grandfather, also John, was responsible for the horse-pulled trams in the city. He can be seen at the reins of the first tram.

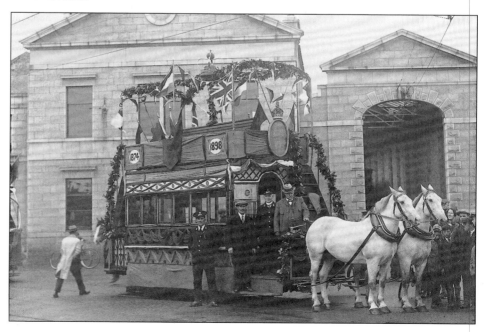

One of Aberdeen's most eminent Victorians in the passenger seat of what was probably the first car in the city in 1898. The Panhard is a true 'horseless carriage' with a footboard like those used to help the reigning in of horses, and carriage lights. It was, of course, before number plates were issued. The passenger, and owner, of the car is William Jackson. The picture was taken outside his home at Thorngrove, Mannofield, which is said to be the first house in Aberdeen to have electricity. Jackson was born on a farm near Inverurie in 1849 and went to India to work in the tea industry for the Scottish Assam Tea Co. When the company centralised its processing operation Jackson designed the machines which were used. He was so successful in this that between 1879 and 1909 he applied for 40 patents for his inventions and the price of tea tumbled from 11d (just under 5p) a pound to under 3d (just over 1p). With over 8,000 of his machines in operation by 1913 Jackson was a wealthy man, but he never forgot his homeland and established an engineering workshop at Thorngrove. His faith in the abilities of his own apprentices was one of the reasons so many North-east men found lucrative careers in the tea industry. William Jackson died in 1915 leaving half his estate, after personal bequests, to set up a chair of engineering at Aberdeen University and half to charities in Calcutta.

Strathdon doctor P. E. Howie, left, sitting proudly in a Daimler in Alford in 1896. The importance of this picture of one of the very earliest cars in the North-East can be judged by the fact that sitting on the right is Dr Otto Meyer, chief engineer of the Daimler car company. Mike Ward of Grampian Transport Museum is now certain Dr Howie's car is the original 'demonstrator' which was owned by F. R. Simms who is considered the father of the British motor industry. It is likely this car was used by the then Prince of Wales and also took part in the first road race which started in Paris in 1894.

This car is probably a product of the Aberdonian Caledonian Motor Works. The baby car with the registration SU 25 would have been chugging along North-East roads in the early years of the 20th century. The picture comes from Mrs Isabel Gordon of Kelso who believes it shows her grandparents Mr and Mrs Peter Webster. If that is the case the baby is Mrs Gordon's mother who was born in 1904.

An 1854 picture of the Guild Street station which opened on the site of today's bus station. Note the masts of the nearby ships in the harbour. This station closed in 1867 when the first Joint Station was built. Pictures courtesy of the Great North of Scotland Railway Association.

The age of steam in Aberdeen. This picture from 1912 shows the view looking south from Union Bridge. The Joint Station is being rebuilt with men working on one of the lines. The footbridge from the Palace Hotel which used to stand on Union Street is in the foreground. On the left the site of Hadden's Mills is being converted for sidings. The roof of the old station dominates the background of this picture. The picture illustrates how important rail links had become to Aberdeen in the decades since the first locomotive steamed into the city from the south on 16 March 1850. A fortnight later services to the south from Aberdeen began.

The allure of steam was still alive in 1978 when the 40-year-old *Union of South Africa* pulled into Aberdeen. The privately-owned engine made the trip from Edinburgh in a nostalgic journey which took many people back to 1967 when the last steam engine rolled into the city on a normal service.

The steam powered wagon named *The Tiger* at work around Aberdeen Harbour in 1958 – 34 years after she first hissed her way along the quays. A company spokesman responded with feeling when asked if the old wagon was ready for retirement. "She helps to shift trawlers and railway wagons," he said. "And she can pull really heavy loads. She runs on three bags of coke a day… she needs practically no repairs and isn't in the least temperamental." And as she only ran on Harbour Board property she wasn't taxed. The Super Sentinel RS 5540 is still chugging along to this day after being lovingly restored by Bill Edwards of Culter who bought it in 1964. Bert Stewart who worked on the machine wondered what other road users made of *The Tiger* when they encountered it at night. "It must have looked a fearsome thing on the road with a three-foot plume of flame coming out of the smokestack and 20ft of sparks above that." *The Tiger*, which needs its 350-gallon water tank filled up every 20 miles, is now based in England. Resplendent in its original maroon livery it is valued at around £44,000. Not bad appreciation on a vehicle sold for £250 in 1964.

This picture of a 1920s scooter came courtesy of Bill Jamieson of Bridge of Don, Aberdeen. The picture taken in Aberdeen's Gallowgate was identified by enthusiast William Smith of Bridge of Don as a 1921 Autoglider. The motorised scooter was another idea which started in Britain but was popularised elsewhere. The woman has been identified as Jessie Norman the wife of Jack Forsyth who helped run a family butchery business in the Gallowgate.

The thrill of flight is captured in this 1953 picture of an air display at Dyce. A Canberra flies past low and slow past the crowds. The large aircraft on the runway in the centre of the picture is an Avro Shackleton of RAF Coastal Command. Pictured in the front row are an Avro Anson, Airspeed Oxford, Miles Magister and a second Anson. This picture was taken from the old ATC tower which was demolished in the 1970s.

The steam engine *Dunrobin* at Inverness before being shipped to Canada in 1950. For decades it pulled a courtesy coach to the Duke of Sunderland's home, Dunrobin Castle, from Inverness. Four kings and Kaiser Wilhelm travelled in the tiny cab over the years.

Changing Aberdeen

Washing day in Martins Lane, one of Aberdeen's many crowded tenements huddled together in the city centre in the 1930s. This picture is from 1937 and shows just why these damp buildings with few facilities and outside toilets had to go. The ingenuity of the tenants can be seen in the poles pushed from windows to act as washing lines.

The Welfare House in the Spital was a 1930s symbol of what improved housing should be like for Aberdeen folk. Moving force behind this enlightened development was Dr Mary Esslemont, a doughty fighter for deprived folk. Dr Esslemont's life of achievement was marked in 1981 when the Freedom of Aberdeen was conferred on her. Many *Evening Express* readers wrote in to testify to how happy they were at the house built for the welfare of mothers and children. For people who knew slum conditions the fitted kitchen, inside toilet with window, bedrooms and bathroom were a revelation. A boiler room took care of the hot water. A large loft with staircase allowed easy access to an area for storage and drying laundry. There was even a balcony and a wash-house so large that the 12 families could hold parties in it. Eventually the flats were offered at affordable prices to sitting tenants and sold.

A city's thanks. Dr Mary Esslemont accepts a silver casket from Lord Provost Norman Collie to mark her receiving the Freedom of the City for her lifetime of work to improve the health care and living conditions of Aberdeen folk.

A wintry scene in Loch Street, Aberdeen, in 1970 long before the major changes which have overtaken this area. The school on Loch Street has gone and now the John Lewis superstore and an overhead walkway link with the St Nicholas Centre have changed the area forever.

Beauty amid the squalor as Marischal College is briefly revealed as the Guestrow is demolished in the Thirties. The ornate shining granite of the college makes a stark contrast to the crumbling old buildings in this picture by Leonard Pelman.

The bridges which once spanned Aberdeen Harbour can be seen in this panoramic view from 1962. On the right is the 650-ton Regent Bridge which swung open to allow entrance to the Upper Dock. The bridge, a landmark for 70 years, was demolished in 1974. In the distance is the St Clement's Bridge which was opened by the Queen Mother in 1953 and lasted until 1975.

While the name Lemon Tree lives on through the Aberdeen centre for the arts the bar which gave it its name has long since disappeared. There are references to this popular haunt of the legal profession and reporters as far back as the early 19th century. Our picture shows the Lemon Tree in St Nicholas Street. In earlier days it was situated in Exchequer Row.

Aberdeen's Riverside Drive in 1932 before the King George VI Bridge spanned the Dee. Note the nets from the salmon bothy draped over the railings. The picture was provided by Ernest Thomson of Riverside Drive.

Cheers all round at the opening of Aberdeen's rebuilt New Market on 31 January 1974. The topping out ceremony was led by beauty queen Catherine Robertson and Dons player Willie Young.

Three children on what was known as The Rocky Road. Bill Morrice of Aberdeen who provided the picture said the 'road' ran to Findlay's Farm where children once collected milk and eggs. He says Tullos School is now on the land to the left of this picture.

The dream kitchen of 1959 which *Evening Express* readers had a chance to win. The newspaper offered £200 to buy 'the sort of kitchen you dream about'. The contest blurb adds: 'How easy the cooking and washing would be in a place like this?'

The Life Boys of the 20th Company, Torry United Free Church marching to Mannofield Church in the late Fifties. Led by Captain Fred Freeland they are passing the long gone old Ice Rink on Anderson Drive, Aberdeen.

Muckle Friday at Aberdeen's Castlegate in the 1930s. Among the men seeking farm work can be seen a recruiting sergeant offering a very different form of employment.

The corner of Market Street and Union Street, Aberdeen, in the austere 1930s.

The Crown Street office of Munro's Tourist Agency in 1949 when you could get an air tour to Douglas, Isle of Man, for £10 5s.

Trams rattle past the Palace Hotel in this 1935 picture of Union Street before the luxury hotel was destroyed by fire in 1941.

Tracer horses rest at the foot of Aberdeen's steep Market Street before being hitched on to the next load they will help haul up to Union Street.

A study of The Green in the the early 1930s. The Green Mannie statue was still a centrepiece of Aberdeen's ancient market in those days.

The quiet hamlet of Dyce near Aberdeen in 1930.

Dyce in 1973 as a building boom starts.

Boarding a BEA plane at Dyce airport in 1969.

A plane can be seen on the left of makeshift sheds in this 1960 picture of what grew into a busy international airport at Dyce.

Drama

A spectacular picture from 1948 shows Holburn Street School ablaze after a mystery explosion in the top floor. Built in 1863, the school was extended in 1911. Long running attempts to rebuild the school eventually ended in 1958 and the building was demolished in 1963 for the ill-fated Commercial College to rise on the site. After safety fears the building was abandoned and finally fell to the breakers' ball for a new high-rise building which went up in 2000.

The Aberdeen Harbour sheerpoles after they collapsed in September 1950. One man died when the 95ft high 48-ton tripod crashed to the ground at Waterloo Quay in high winds.

An atmospheric shot of a trawler grounded on the North-East coast and pounded by heavy seas.

A dramatic picture from February 1966 when a goods train derailed near Stonehaven. The fireman of the crashed train raced back along the Aberdeen-Edinburgh line to warn an approaching train of the derailment in a gorge three and a half miles south of Stonehaven.

A stark memorial to an 1883 sea tragedy. *The Queen*, a coal-laden schooner, is stranded on Aberdeen Beach where she was driven in a fierce storm as she tried to make the shelter of the harbour. A number of the crew, nearly senseless from the cold, were blown to their deaths from the ship's rigging as they fought to save the sail ship.

High seas brought the cars out to Aberdeen's Greyhope Road to watch nature's spectacular show. Here the Titan crane is framed against the waves. The crane was one of a pair used to strengthen the south breakwater after the great gale of 1937 tore a 100ft gap in the harbour defences. Work began in 1938, stopped at the outbreak of war, and didn't resume until 1954. The improvements were at the mercy of weather and tides and were not completed until 1965. John Melville was one of the drivers of the pictured crane which was named Goliath. He says: "Being steam powered it was smooth as anything." The work entailed moving 30-ton concrete blocks from a yard near the breakwater where they were made. They were then loaded on a Sentinel steam engine by the first Titan crane and transported to the second crane. The breakwater the men constructed is 1,050ft long, 35ft wide and the lighthouse tower stands 92ft above the high-water mark.

Aberdeen lifeboat sails into a murky harbour on placid waters in December, 1937. It is the end of a year which began with one of the fiercest storms ever to batter the North-East coast. Between 21 January and 1 February the gales were so bad that one of the harbour breakwaters was washed away. The city's lifeboat *Emma Constance* was called out three times, most notably on 26 January when the coastal steamer *Fairey* was drifting towards heavy surf north of Aberdeen. The lifeboat stood by the steamer despite being repeatedly swept by the waves and eventually saved all the crew who jumped to safety when the lifeboat pulled alongside. One crewman fell between the lifeboat and the steamer but was bravely grabbed by lifeboatman John Masson who pulled him to safety.

An early use of the helicopter to get a patient to hospital in Aberdeen.

Great Events

At lunchtime on 9 February 1942, a Luftwaffe JU88 on a sea-level attacking run towards Aberdeen was destroyed by two patrolling Spitfires. The Spitfires flown by sergeants Prytherch and Rowson were from 603 Squadron and a few days later they had an official Press Day at Dyce where this picture was taken. All members who intercepted the Nazi plane participated. Thanks to war history enthusiast James C. Milne of Balgownie Road, Aberdeen, for this information. Jim points out that the actions of these brave airmen undoubtedly saved the city from strafing or bomb damage but there is no permanent memorial at the airport to its wartime role in offence, defence and training.

The 4th Gordon's, the City of Aberdeen's own, pictured together in France in 1939, only a month after the war had started. This territorial battalion had been stationed at Woolmanhill Barracks. The picture came from George Milne of Bucksburn, Aberdeen, who recalls that although he was a member of the 4th Gordons he was kept back in Aberdeen as he was a Boy Soldier. He says: "I then volunteered for the Commandos and did not rejoin my regiment but was proud in my Army career to carry the 4th

The men and women of the Woodside Air Raid Patrol group pose for a picture at St John's Hall with their rattles, hand bells and stirrup pumps laid in front of them. Bob Hunter, 74, the warden on the extreme right of the front row sent in this picture which was taken in 1942. The ARP were an essential part of wartime life ensuring the blackout curtains allowed no chink of light out to aid enemy aircraft. The rattles and bells were intended for alerting the public to air raids and the stirrup pumps just may have helped to put out some small fires. In 1943 Bob left the ARP and went to Italy to serve with the Queen's Own Cameron Highlanders.

The brave battle veterans of the Boer War pose for a picture at the Gordon Barracks. These members of the Aberdeen branch of the South African War Association lined up outside the Gordon Barracks in 1936, some 37 years after the outbreak of that war. Mrs Harriet Ellis's father, Alexander Sutherland Innes (seventh right on the front row) was a founder of the association. Mr Innes, who died in 1941 aged 61 was conscripted into the Army and shipped to South Africa after he was orphaned as a young lad. He spent most of his life in the Army, latterly in the War Pensions Office.

An excited crowd gather around bomb damage in Craigie Street, Aberdeen, after an overnight raid. Clive Barclay of Bridge of Don provided the picture which shows his mother Polly Barclay (née Upton) holding the lump of plaster. Isabel Shepherd (née Johnston) is also in the picture and remembers that incident in 1943 vividly. She wrote: "The big air raid began at around 9pm when an aircraft came in from the Torry area, machine gunned up George Street and dropped bombs on Gordon's College, Old George Street School (later to become the Trades College), and a mason's yard at the back of 20 to 24 Craigie Street. The Luftwaffe aircraft then targeted Broadford Works, Hutcheon Street and Charles Street before heading out to sea. The windows and their frames and the walls between the rooms at 20 to 24 Craigie Street were blown out and the picture shows some of that damage being cleared up."

Saving Private Rennie. A welcome home for Pte Norman Rennie at Aberdeen's YMCA Station Canteen. The two girls are Molly Bews, left, formerly of Cults and Georgina Grieve the late aunt of Irene Rose of Stonehaven who submitted this picture. It was the first repatriation of World War Two Prisoners of War to Aberdeen. Norman's sister Mrs E. McKay of Pittodrie, Aberdeen, was present and recalls the girls in

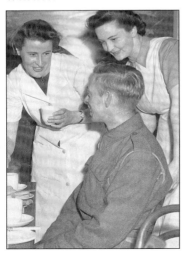

the picture kept putting more and more sugar into Norman's cup while waiting for the picture to be taken. She also revealed her brother's remarkable story. Pte Rennie had been hit in the back by shrapnel and left for dead. For a day and a half he lay gravely ill, the strange noise the hole in his back made when he coughed – as though someone was imitating him – became a focus of his fight to stay alive. After 36 hours he was laid on a death cart. Two medical helpers, Bert Gardiner and James Fraser, were checking for life holding mirrors to the casualties to see if they were breathing. As they checked Pte Rennie he suddenly opened his eyes and startled the pair. They helped nurse Norman back to health. He was at various PoW camps, finally being repatriated from the salt mines in Poland. Norman married a girl named Isobel and they set up home in Montrose. He worked as an engineer and after retirement the couple moved to Forfar. Norman died in 1987 and Isobel died in Kintore in 1998.

Pictures of the unsung lumberjack heroes of World War Two in the Memories column of the *Evening Express* created a big reaction with many letters – some from across the Atlantic. The first pictures were sent by Gene Ivor Williams of Glithno, by Stonehaven, who explained that after 1940 the loss of imported timber from Russia and Scandinavia meant Britain had to rely on its own timber. With most young men involved in the war effort there weren't enough workers to fell the trees. Canada was asked to help and adverts were placed for professional lumberjacks to be trained as soldiers. The response was good and 20 companies of 200 men arrived in Scotland. The men were great characters and were very popular in the areas they worked – Aboyne, Inverness, Black Isle, Culloden, Kincraig, Braemar, Banchory, Brechin.

The shortage of men also led to the formation of companies of lumberjills. In 1942 around 300 of the new Women's Land Army Timber Corps went to work in forests across the North-East. These were one of Britain's secret weapons, women from all walks of life doing the jobs of men serving in the forces. Park House at Drumoak was one of the Lumberjill academies where they gained the skills and fitness to fell timber in a five-week course. The wage for girls over 19 was 2/6 (12.5p) a week. Aberdeen's wartime Lord Provost Sir Thomas Mitchell told the lumberjills in 1944: "But for you the country and the fighting forces would have been much worse off." This information comes from the book *Timber*, the wartime memories of Affleck Gray which were completed by his daughter Uiga Robertson of Kingussie along with her son. The book was published by the Tuckwell Press. Photograph from The Bonny Macadam Collection.

In wartime everyone had to make do the best they could. That applied to these fellows of the Army Cadet Force at their annual camp in 1943. They were used to being looked after by the Army Catering Corps, but with the Catering Corps in Europe looking after the troops the boys had to look after themselves. So cadets from all over the North-East gathered in Aberdeen for this intensive cookery course. Norman Duncan of Cults, one of the young caterers in the picture, can still remember the outcome of the cooking at that year's camp in Ballater – he was violently sick.

Marching off to war down Union Street on 9 October 1939. Among the soldiers is George Milne, 79, of Kincorth, Aberdeen. George told us the men were bound for Aldershot led by Captain Eric Munro, Lieut Robert Maitland, Company Sgt Maj Pat 'Kiltie' Mathieson and Sgt John Black. The men returned to Aberdeen on leave in December 1939 before going to France in 1940. After Dunkirk they made a forced march to Le Havre where an expected rearguard action never happened. The men – then part of the 51st Arc Force made up of the troops not killed or captured at St Valery – returned to Cherbourg to escape back to Britain as the Nazis entered the town on 16 June 1940.

Off to war they go, marching down Union Street in 1939. The camera captures the moment some friends waved goodbye.

Pride in the rain. Bad weather fails to dampen the enthusiasm of theses mums with their offspring at a mother and baby competition in Aberdeen in August, 1944. Picture courtesy of Frances Park of Aberdeen.

A captured German U-boat goes on display at Aberdeen Harbour in 1945.

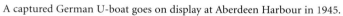

It's 1945 and time to take down the bricks which protected Aberdeen's newspaper office from bomb damage.

Artillery training when Aberdeen's Torry Battery still protected the city from any threat coming from the sea.

Huge crowds queue up to visit a Royal Navy ship at Aberdeen Harbour not long before the outbreak of World War Two.

Regal Deeside

The railway gives up at Ballater with a sigh of relief. This is the railhead station for Balmoral. All the notabilities of the Victorian Era and a good many of the Edwardian and the Georgian have stepped down on its platform. Guards of honour have often been posted outside the ticket office. Distinguished parcels are, throughout the autumn, carried tenderly from luggage vans.

H.V. Morton, *In Search of Scotland*, 1929.

While pictures of royalty are probably never truly lost to the public gaze, there is a time when they gather dust. Hidden for a while.

That is the case of the collection on the following pages, taken originally from decaying boxes containing glass slides and with labels like '1922-27 Royalty'.

The *Aberdeen Journal's* photographers have had an unrivalled opportunity to record the lives and times of our royalty.

Since Queen Victoria's era, Balmoral Castle on Deeside has been a central part of the royals' lives.

And as the years passed, the moments captured in those routine diary chores of the photographers took on a special significance.

Several times a year, as the famous travel writer H. V. Morton noted, the nobility called on Ballater as it headed for Balmoral.

Even the standard inspection of the guard outside Ballater railway station became piquant as the Princes grew up and became Kings.

And Princess Elizabeth can, in these pictures, be seen finding a maturity and gathering the assurance of a monarch.

So behind these mundane day-to-day duties of the royals on Deeside and in Aberdeen there were always great events unfolding secretly. Some of these were events which shook the nation.

The Prince of Wales at the laying of the foundation stone for Aberdeen's new hospital at Foresterhill on 28 August 1928.

The Prince of Wales followed by the Duke of Gloucester and the Lord Provost of Aberdeen after the laying of the foundation stone for Aberdeen Royal Infirmary at Foresterhill.

The general scene showing the platform and the large invited crowd at Foresterhill for the foundation stone ceremony. Note the orchestra beside the platform steps.

The Prince of Wales strides past the nurses' guard of honour during the laying of the foundation stone ceremony for the hospital at Foresterhill in 1928.

The Duke and Duchess of York at the official opening of Aberdeen Royal Infirmary in 1936 as the abdication storm clouds began to gather. It was 23 September and the new King Edward VIII was expected to officially open the hospital he had laid the foundation stone for. Instead he met divorcee Mrs Wallis Simpson at Aberdeen's railway station while his younger brother and his wife took over his official duty. Before the year was out, Edward VIII abdicated to marry Mrs Simpson.

Queen Mary at Ballater station in 1925 after arriving on the royal train from Aberdeen bound for Balmoral Castle.

The Prince of Wales at Ballater after travelling along the Deeside railway line. With him on this September day in 1925 is the Duke of Kent.

The Prince of Wales shakes hands with a Gordon Highlander at their camp in 1925.

The Prince of Wales at Ballater in 1927.

The baby looking out at a curious world from her pram is Princess Elizabeth. Behind the nurse at this visit to the Balmoral Fête on Deeside in 1927 is Queen Mary and behind her at the side of King George V is the proud mother, the Duchess of York. The Duke of York is behind the King.

The Prince of Wales is caught unawares by a photographer on the road to Crathie Church on 8 September 1930. Also in the carriage on a rainy day are King George V and Queen Mary. Beside the Prince of Wales is the Duke of Gloucester.

King George V leaving Crathie Church, close by Balmoral Castle, after the service on Sunday in 1932.

The Duke and Duchess of York take their children, Princess Elizabeth and Princess Margaret to the Crathie Fête in 1933.

Princess Elizabeth with her mother and grandmother, and King George V can just be seen raising his hand in acknowledgement of the crowd in this Crathie run picture from 1933.

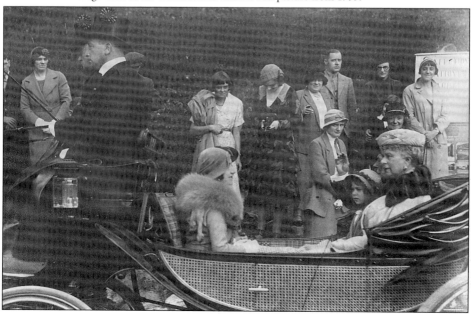

The royal party arrive at the Braemar Gathering in 1933.

The Prince of Wales inspecting the guard of honour at Ballater in 1933.

King George V and the Prince of Wales at Ballater in 1934.

Queen Mary, the young Princesses and the Duke and Duchess of York are welcomed to the 1934 Braemar Gathering.

This carriage at Crathie in 1935 carries a King, a young man destined to be King and two women who will be Queens – Princess Elizabeth, the Duke and Duchess of York and King George V.

Smiling through the rain, the Duchess of York is sheltered by an umbrella on a visit to Aberdeen Girl Guides in 1935.

The Duchess of York with her daughters Princess Elizabeth and Princess Margaret at a birthday party at Elsick House on 23 September 1935.

Princess Elizabeth, centre, and Princess Margaret at a young friend's sixth birthday party at Elsick House in 1935.

Queen Elizabeth visiting Kingseat Naval Hospital, Aberdeen, in March 1940.

Queen Elizabeth presents the Black Watch with their colours at Balmoral on 4 September 1937.

George VI and his Queen with Princesses Elizabeth and Margaret in a horse and carriage on Deeside on 4 September 1938.

Queen Elizabeth with her young daughters and the minister at Crathie at the church sale of work in 1938.

The Duke of Kent at Fraserburgh aboard a herring boat on 14 July 1939.

The Duke of Kent meets Buchan lifeboatmen in 1939.

The Duke of Kent at a fish-curing yard in Peterhead in July 1939.

'Under the spreading chestnut tree'. The royal family join in the Scout song with actions at the King's Camp at Abergeldie in the August of 1939.

Rapt attention from the Queen, Princess Elizabeth and Princess Margaret during one of the events at the King's Camp, Abergeldie in 1939.

King George VI and Queen Elizabeth meet World War Two first aid volunteers at Aberdeen in 1941.

The King and Queen meet north east seamen in March 1941. The royal couple are accompanied by Aberdeen Lord Provost Tommy Mitchell.

The Duke of Kent chats to workers at a Peterhead fish house in May, 1941.

Princess Elizabeth inspects Sea Rangers in Aberdeen on 3 October 1944.